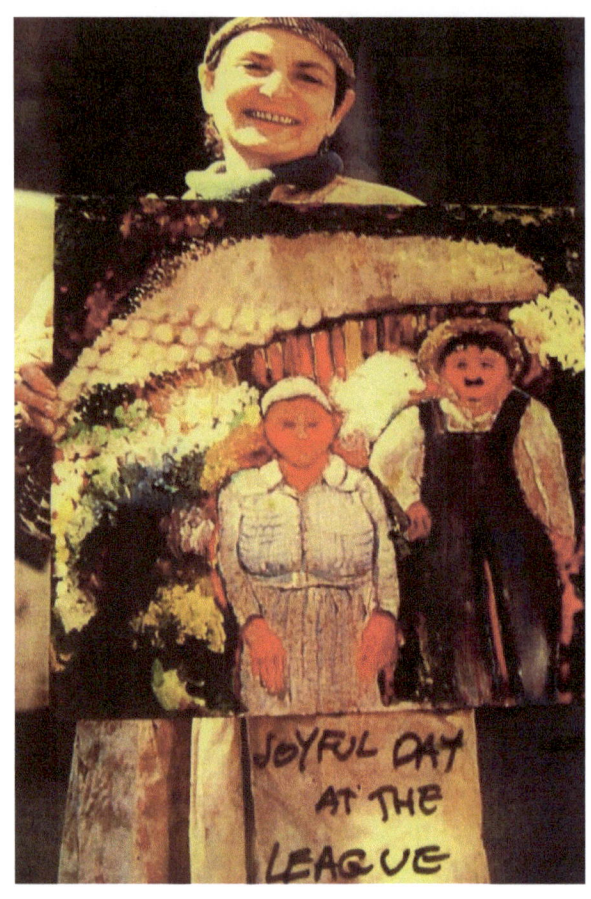

Alice Lived Here

Each Artist has a time in Woodstock. A few moments in Alice Jaffe's Woodstock

By Donna White-Davis© 2018

Alice Lived Here

Each Artist has a time in Woodstock. A few moments in Alice Jaffe's Woodstock

By Donna White-Davis© 2018

I first met Alice on a freezing cold winter's day. I had moved to Woodstock that Fall to fulfill a photograph gallery internship at the Center for Photography in 2001. I knew I could photograph a little, paint a little, write a little, and like most comers to Woodstock was at a transition point in my life. Alice was at a critical in her life. She and her long term significant other Bill were struggling on their way home from the health food store with groceries, shopping cart stuck in the snow and ice, he trying to free the cart, she sitting despondently on the snowbank looking quite lost. I stopped, put the groceries and the cart in my Jeep, helped them in and drove them home. That is the way many Woodstock friendships begin. In Woodstock people just automatically help each other. That has happened always, even before the almost 125 years as Americas first artist colony, Byrdcliffe into the early beginnings of the farms and village people whose descendent still welcome creative people. Alice was one of those people. Her stories will be told, I am confident, by her loving daughters. They will know the story deeper and longer and with greater emotions and complexity. I am not writing her life. I am just writing her time in Woodstock during the time I was there.

Understand Alice and you will get a deeper understanding of the Woodstock ethic of creation.

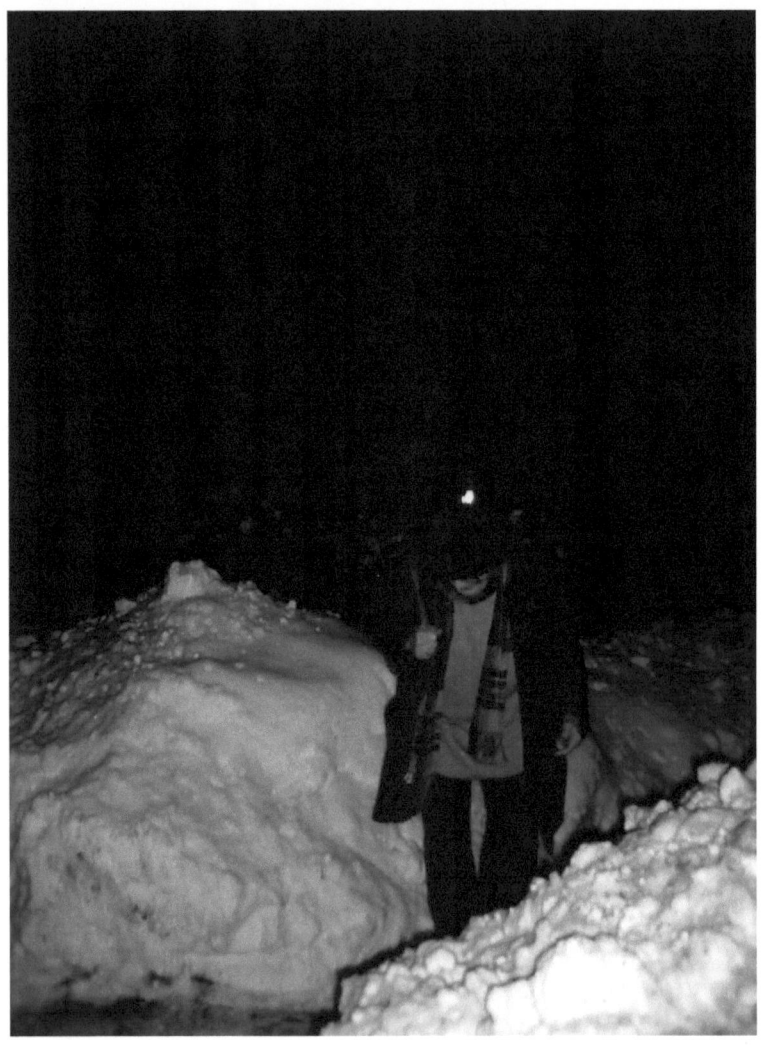

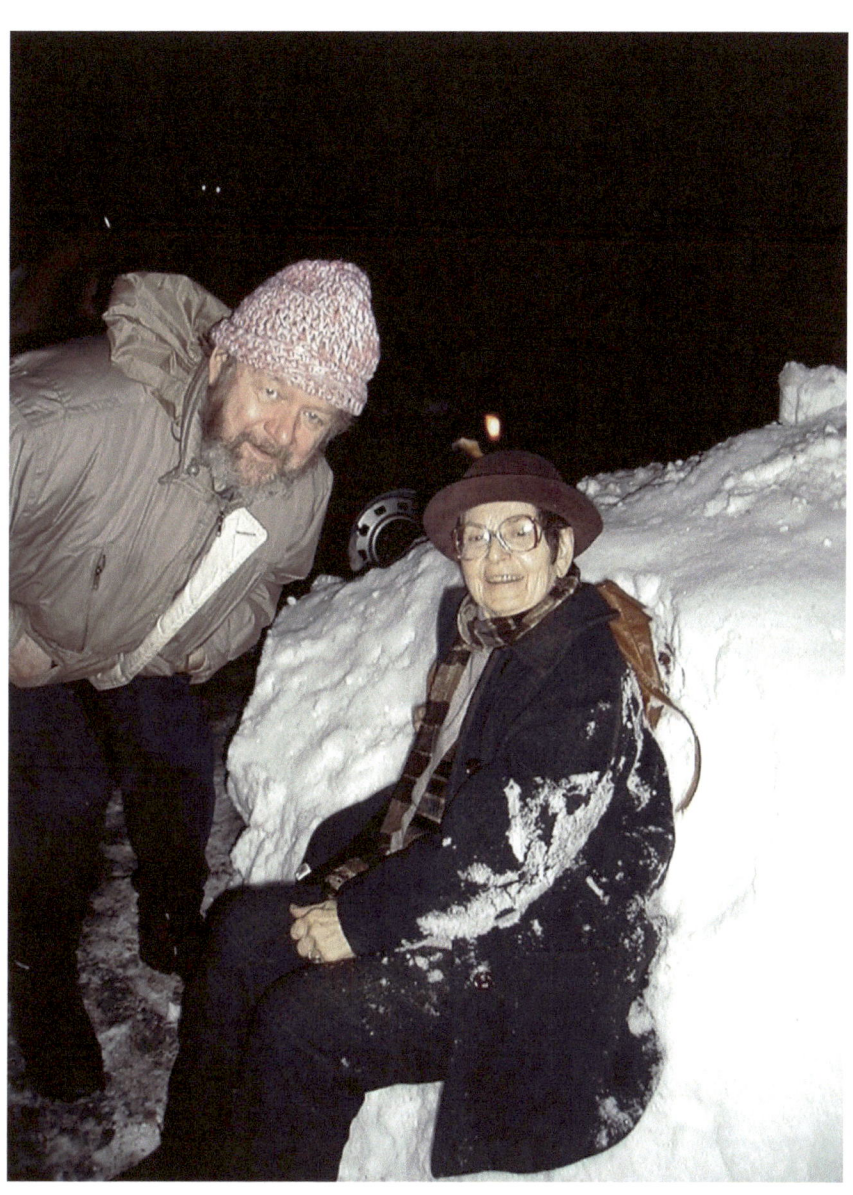

Alice and Bill were in their 70's at the time I met them. The were loving and supportive of each other. They also were forgiving of each other's past. Although privacy is important to Woodstock artists, their story needs to be told because it speaks of the love acceptance and open mindedness that is centuries old in the village. I don't know the complete story. I know the story as they shared it with me. In Woodstock that is all that is needed to know a friend. Their story. Alice had a traditional life married on Long Island to a successful architect with two daughters. Seemingly happy, she felt her own avenues for creativity narrowed by the conventions of the 50's and 60's. Somehow, she was drawn to develop her art at the Arts Student League, the oldest art school in the USA and connected at the time to the Woodstock School of Art. She took course. The married separated. Her love for her daughters and her family never left. She held precious photos of her children and grandchildren in her little studio home alone the Tannery Brook. Throughout our friendship she was writing. She felt compelled to write because she had just been diagnosed with breast cancer, and she was trying to decide how to treat it. Her daughter was a physician and recommended a vigorous treatment. Alice, a student of natural healing was researching alternatives. She was scared but determined to choose her own path. I learned of this one night around 1 am she called me hysterically panicking and so, being in Woodstock I drove over and took her for a ride through the Catskill mountains where we could talk, cry or, her choice, scream in rage at the disease.

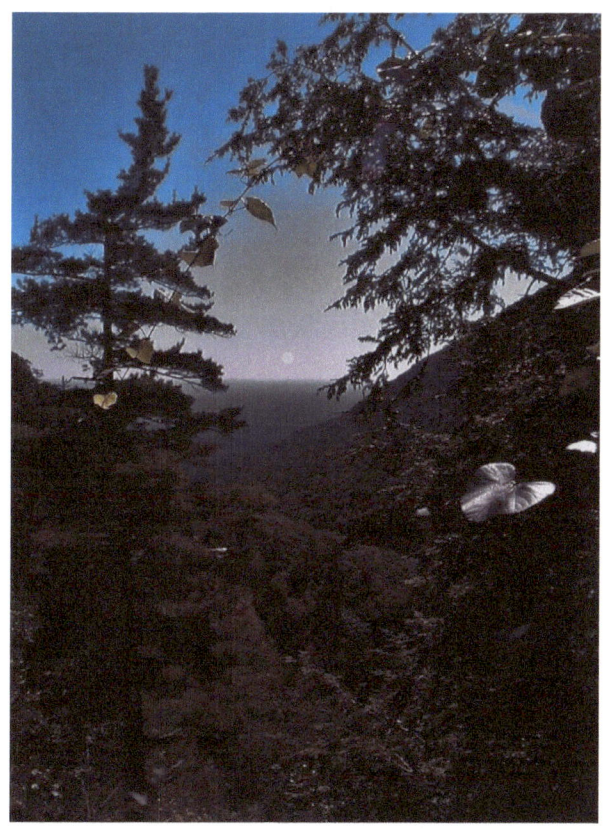

Recognize that point? There are those who believe that was inspiration for Asher Durand's "Kindred Spirits " dedicated to Thomas Cole's. Without either of us knowing, we were driving through the same territory Cole, the founder of the Hudson River School of Art, and Durand walked in, finding the initial inspirations for their sublime paintings.

Well, Alice cleared her psyche and started on her journey of managing her diagnosis while making her artistic life in Woodstock vibrant. Many artists have lived their time in Woodstock, some famous, some unknown all contributing to the tapestry that has become America's art and affected the world. I know that this story isn't "definitive" of Alice's life. It is just a very brief time I shared wither. I and 70 now. I understand with better compassion what Alice's was going through and I want her time and journey to be noted. She deserves that although she would have never tried for fame herself. Hers was a beautiful private contribution to the good created by artists in the world at that time.

In the Woodstock tradition of passing it on, it wasn't long before spring came and Alice offered to take me to see a beautiful field that many experiences following the festival (in Bethel an hour away) camp among the field wild flowers, welcomed by the villagers. In Spring the field is abloom with Mountain laurel, delicate, fragrant, soothing, healing and beautiful.

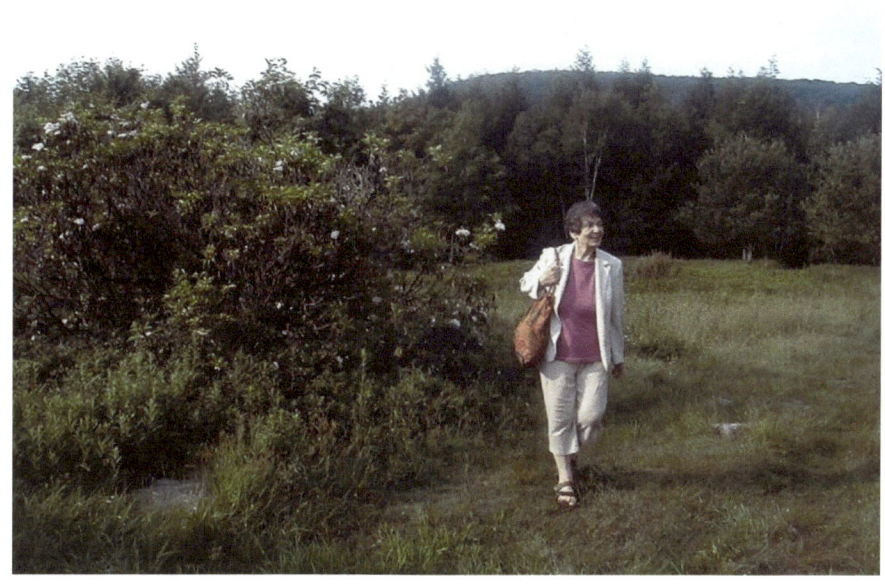

Few years later we were invited to exhibit our paintings with other village artists at the Colony, a music venue and gallery of some renown. For me it was a rare privilege with some degree of actual acceptance that I was an Artist. For Alice it was a recognition that the life choices she made were valued as was her art.

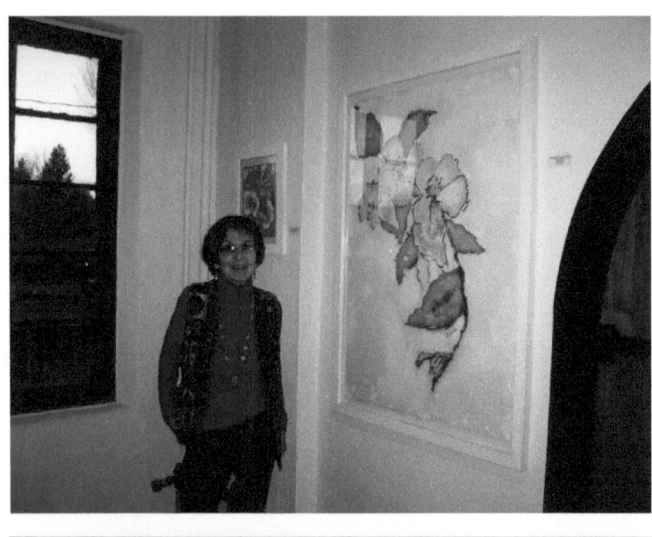
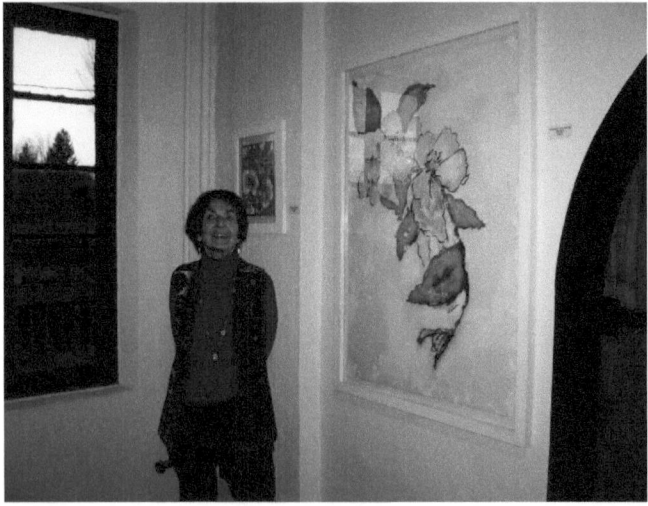

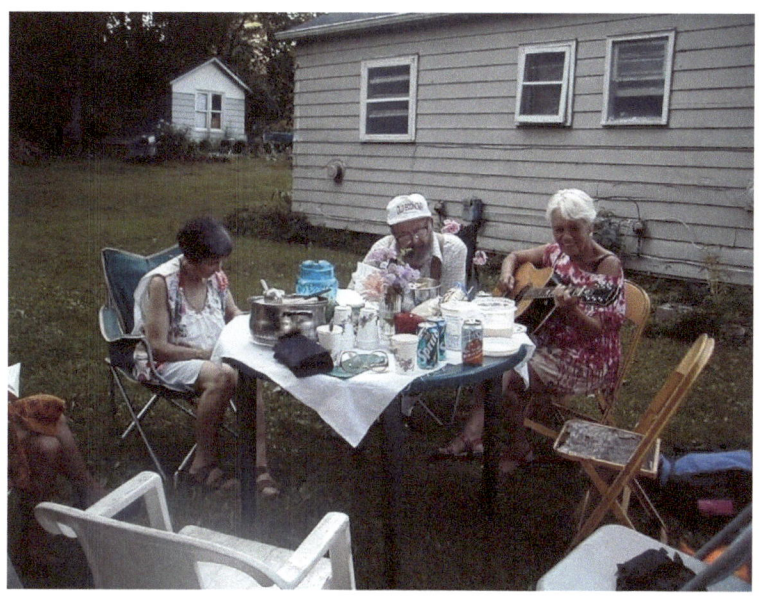

Occasionally Alice would invite me to an impromptu concert in someone yard.

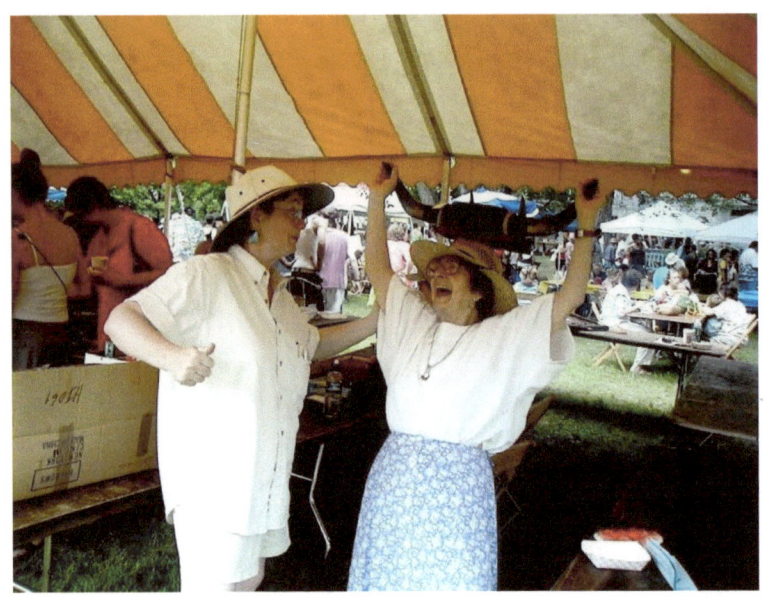

Or a time-honored tradition of the Woodstock Library Fair where she volunteered and gave joy to the atmosphere of art with fun for artists of all ages, especially the children.

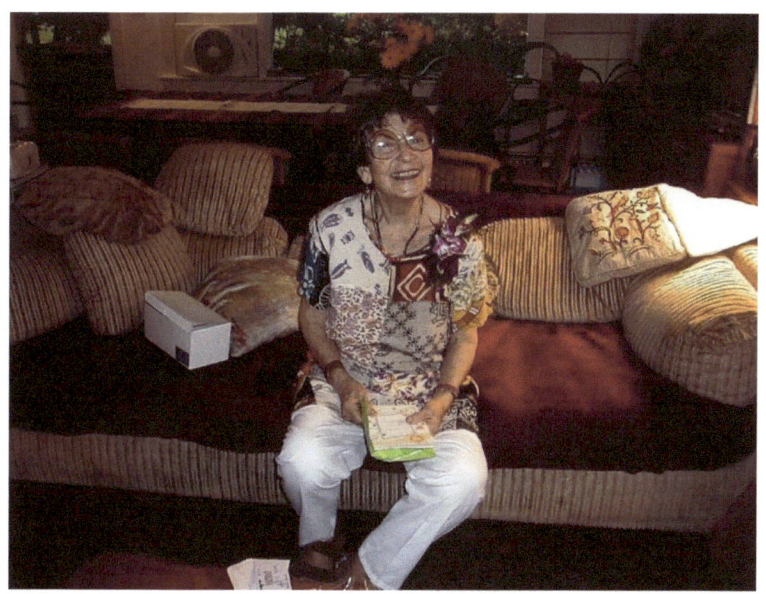

She was approaching her 80th birthday and shared with me her writings of a life journal that, I believe, her daughters now share. It was full of her writings illustrated by Chagall-like illustrations. She loved Chagall and, although developing her own style, felt close to his artistic style. Her family came from Europe early in the 20th century and they had lost many, many members in the Holocaust. She felt that living through that had made family relationship sometimes difficult and that her decisions to follow her art once her children were grown was not valued by siblings.

As with all artists, I don't know the complete story, the secrets, we all have them. I know the story she gave me and that is enough. However, she loved them completely and forgave. One night she called and told me she wanted to take her the next day to Long Island to visit her brother. Of course, we spontaneously took off on an adventure that gave both of us but especially Alice and her brother a memory held for a lifetime and beyond. They also shared time by the ocean, always needed by mountain artists.

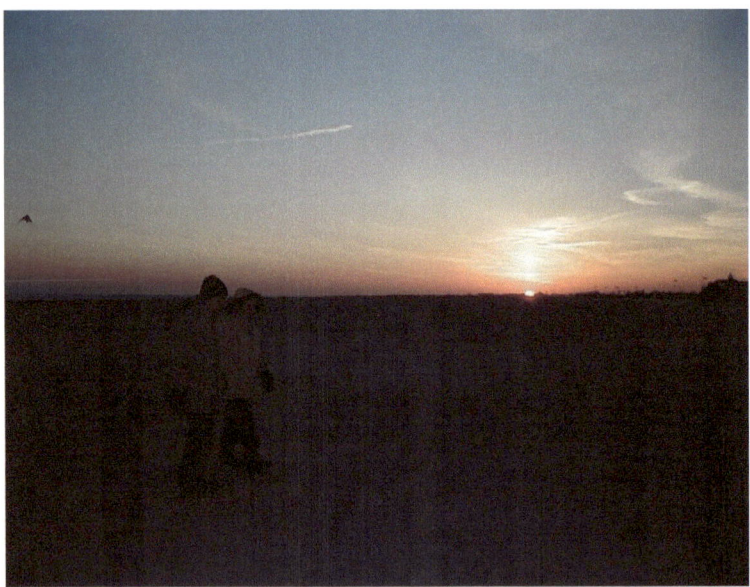

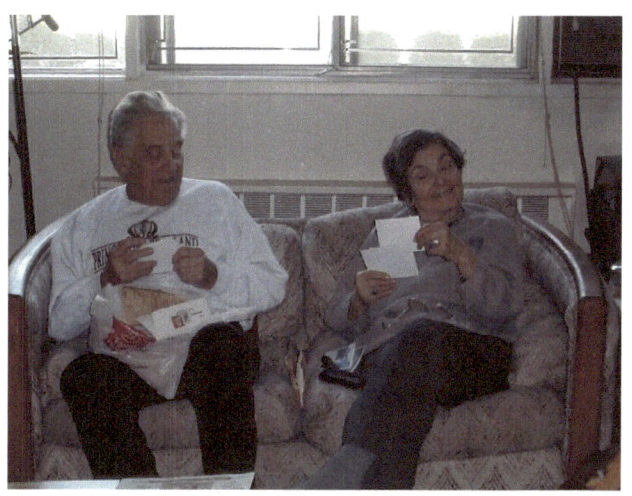

Sharing family photos that meant so much to a family who had lost so much.

She worked hard at her writing with a writing coach who invited her and his other student to present readings at the Kleinert Theater of the Byrdcliffe Guild. All her friends cheered her on.

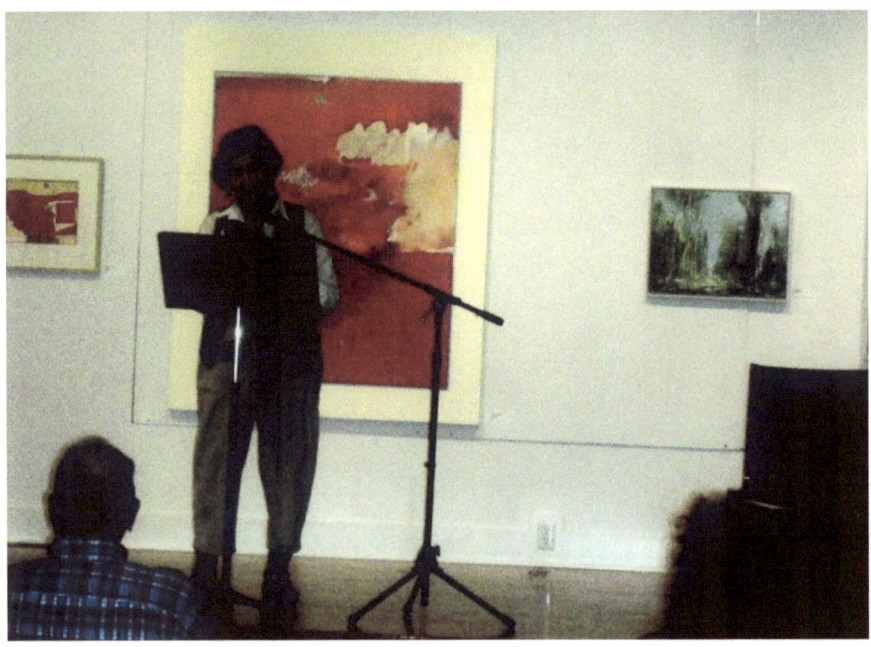

I began augmenting my art with teaching at the public school after undergoing what I believe was an informal and clever screening for values needed to teach young artistic lives and to keep harm from them. I also became certified as a volunteer EMT that limited to my time spent with Alice, but I have no doubt that I would not have done either had my values and healthy life habits been explored by Alice first. She was a gatekeeper.

Alice's 80th birthday was approaching and so she planned for all of us a party with another beautiful artistic experience. Her dear friend provided authentic Indian cooking and gave lessons in making Indian food using the secret combination of spices that the cook's grandmother prepared just for her. We all gathered around the kitchen in Alice's kitchen making flat bread from flour and oil and water exclusively and watching as it bubbled in the fry pan golden brown and delicious, something to this day I use in cooking.

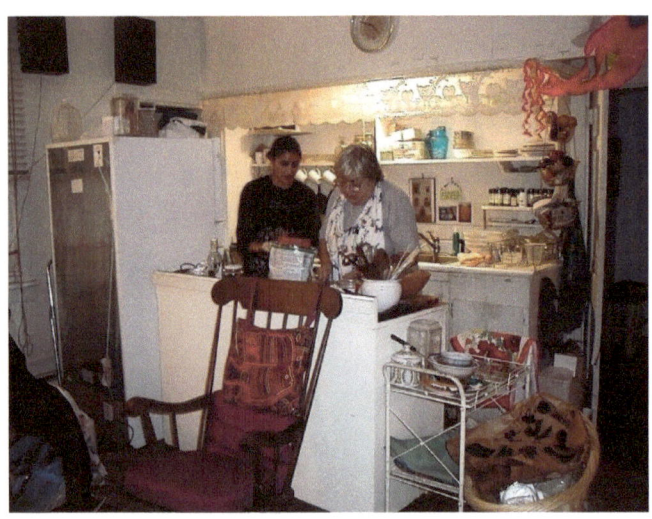

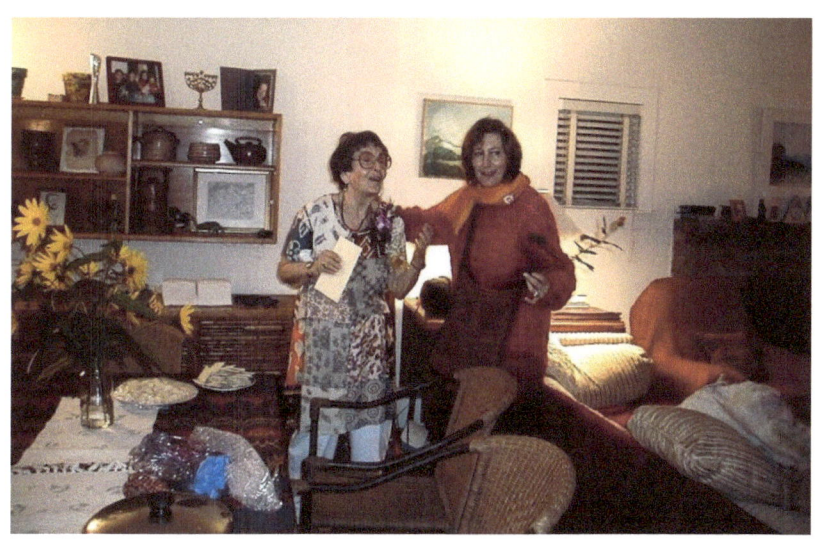

In the Woodstock Artists way. Alice celebrated her 80 years by giving all of us a present.

Bill

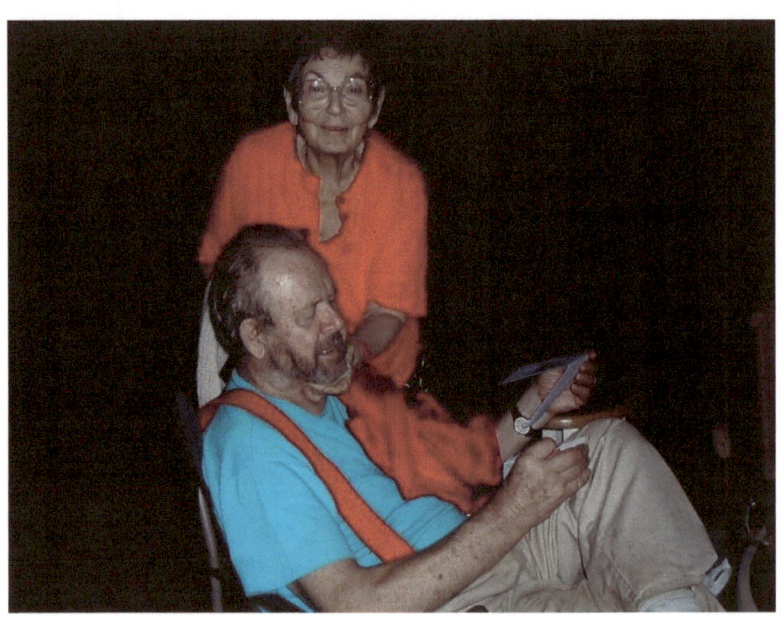

Who was Bill? Alice lived among famous artists.

She knew them. The biographer of Jazz musician Coltrane was her next-door neighbor. Alice had a full social life with many artist and musicians knowing her, but she had a particularly compassionate loving relationship with Bill. Bill is also a Woodstocker who would have gone unknown. I loved to play chess with him, which he prided himself with his strategy having been a military man in the Army Airforce. Does that surprise you? I shouldn't. From the first World War to their time following the Viet Nam War Woodstock has both created to build peace while respecting and support the need for defense. They all now to create free, defense is sometimes needed so they welcome with a literally healing love those harmed during their time defending America. From stories of the artist during World War II manning the fire towers on Overlook Mountain high about the Byrdcliff Artist Colony, looking for enemy aircraft artist and villagers alike took their shifts, familiarizing themselves with the makes and types and flight patterns of aircraft and how to report any possible risks. Does that seem inconsistent with your idea of "Woodstock"? It shouldn't. Creative genius often has the ability to hold two opposing ideas in their mind at the same time trying to find a unique answer to a crisis. So, it goes. It wasn't until many years later, I learned that Bill actually was on the plane that brought the Atomic Bomb to Japan, a truth that cause him haunted nights and a sense often of guilt and unrest. Ironically, among Alice's friends was also a Japanese Artist in Japan at the time of the bombing, both sharing a glass of wine, not talking just forgiving. That also is Woodstock.

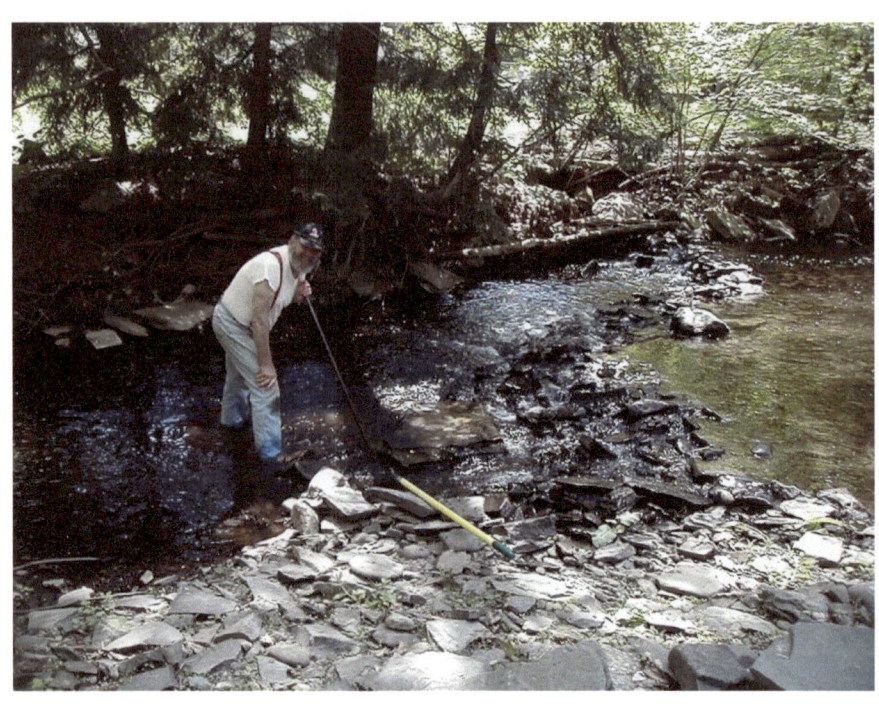

Bill clearing the stream behind Alice's studio.

Now Alice has passed. Her spirit is still in the mountains above the village. I had moved from Woodstock, my life never travelled in straight lines either, And I was told she had passed. I know she is blessed with God. After the war, I know like many of us she struggled with faith, exploring all beliefs that would bring her the sense of fairness we all seek. She is with God. I just wanted you all to know who she was while sharing time with Woodstock Artists. One realizes fast that when we meet in other times, in other places and have the one place, Woodstock, in common there is a mysticism we shar of creation and place but not always shared memories. I found joy in walking from what I called my 'Teenie Weenie "studio" by the Millstream into the village and finding is a panoply of change. Depending upon the event, the time of music and often just who was in the village, the colors sights and sounds changed. I am giving you a little taste of Alice's time, so we won't ever forget Alice Lived Here.

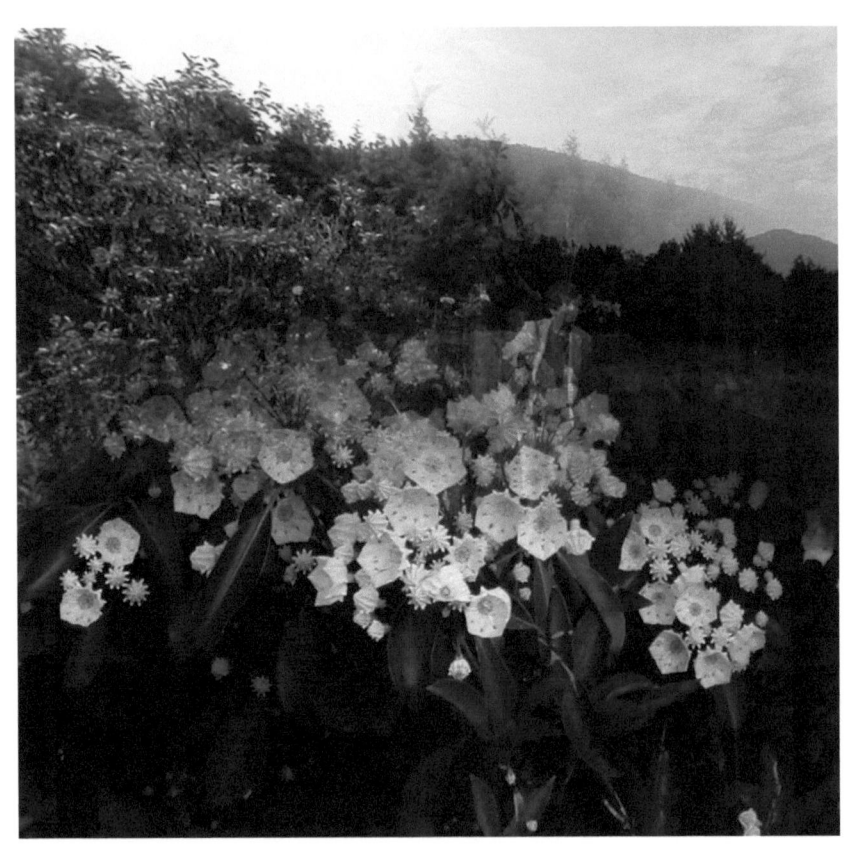

Dedicated to artists all over the world who love Woodstock.

Alice Jaffe 9/17/23-12/7/10

My heartfelt gratitude for all who made my life in Woodstock possible giving me the opportunity to have the Art Spirit touch me. I love you in countless quiet ways.

Photography copyright Donna White-Davis 2002-2009

www.ingramcontent.com/pod-product-compliance
Lightning Source LLC
Chambersburg PA
CBHW041945240526
45473CB00033B/610